VERNON

A VISITOR'S GUIDE OF

HOW NOT TO
SAIL
THE

GREEK ISLES

AND OTHER MINOR CATASTROPHES

**BURDEN FREE
READING**

FOR
SAILBOAT
AND FERRYBOAT
SAILORS

VERNON VAS ELLIOTT

A VISITOR'S GUIDE OF
HOW NOT TO
SAIL

the

and other minor catastrophes

FOR SAILBOAT OR FERRYBOAT SAILORS

Efstathiadis Group S.A.
Agiou Athanasiou Street,
GR - 145 65 Anixi, Attikis

ISBN 960 226 492 6

Printed and bound in Greece by Efstathiadis Group S.A.

Vernon Elliott

to all kindred spirits at sea
and on land
who were unfortunate enough
to cross my path
while sailing the Greek Isles
or anywhere else for that matter

also to any sailor
who ever had his sail torn

The Greeks are an enthusiastic, curious minded, passionate people. Passion, contradictoriness, confusion, chaos, all those sterling human qualities I rediscovered and cherished again.
And generosity.

Henry Miller, *The Colossus of Maroussi*

PRELUDE

A long standing fantasy among daring and not so daring souls is to get on a sailboat and sail into the sunset leaving the rat race behind.

A premier destination in this fantasy is the Greek Isles, those sun drenched, little dots in the Aegean Sea, with the sparkling white, picturesque villages on them, where life is simple, donkeys roam the streets, natives are friendly and the discos' sounds not too loud.

Well, I did it. Matter of fact I'm still doing it and it still is a fantasy because the disco sounds in many places are indeed too loud.

In the course of the Odyssey, unpredictable and fascinating things happen. This is a small account of some of these things and some other things that might be interesting, informative or just amusing, whether you are contemplating or dreaming of such a venture or not, painted with the......pigments of my imagination. For your amusement.

Vernon

CONTENTS

SAILING

Henry Beard and Roy McKie defined sailing as the fine art of getting wet and becoming ill while slowly going nowhere at a great expense. All of it true. Sailing is a madness, an all consuming madness, a lunacy and a fine art and a fine madness it is.

Nothing is as exhilarating to the ones afflicted and possessing the talent, as to leave port, set sails, turn the damned motor off and glide away to the sounds of sea and wind and sun. Nothing. Destination is of secondary importance. The sailor moves in time not in space. A few hours of joy is the destination. Away from the din of the city, away from the rat race, from screaming children, nagging wives, acid rock and acid rain, Balkan wars, away from reality and into the heavens. For a few hours, same as eternity. A master of your own destiny. That's the destination.

At 4,5,6,7,8 knots per hour, you are slowly going nowhere and everywhere.

Well, in Greece you add another dimension to the madness. A destination in space. Over 3000 islands and only a handful inhabited, about 170 or so they say. And all very close. What else can a man ask for? Wind, sparkling clear water, bright, warm, hospitable sun and colorful, romantic isles and coves and warm summer evenings and moonlit nights. Wow.

And the MELTEMI, the only hitch in the idyllic scenario. And what a hitch it is! Late July and all of August this monster wind brings home the real meaning of the Beard-McKie definition of "getting wet and becoming ill". The Meltemi is a strong, gusty wind, usually N or NE or NW but unpredictably so, that sweeps the Aegean and is more vicious around the Cyclades, the central part of the Sea. It is not difficult to negotiate, it is almost impossible at times. It reaches 45 knot speeds and has swirling gusts of 50 to 55 at times, which is by no means pleasant sailing conditions. And it could last for days on end keeping you and your boat in port. It's not the wind alone but the damn waves as well. They are short and choppy and high at the same time. ...and besides all that, the moment you think that you are reaching land and safety and rest, you are hit by the phenomenal SPILIADES, the swirling and totally unpredictable, forceful gusts, off of the lee side of the island, affected by the contours of the mountainsides. But also on the windward side as well. No rest for the afflicted with the sailing bug. None for the wicked, either.

What to do? Particularly when you are neither a masochist nor congenitally insane and you value your life. A little bit anyway.

There are solutions, despair not! You choose the early summer months, May and June are good ones and so are the late summer months of September and October. As I sit writing this, it is October 25th, it's a wonderful, bright day with the temperatures in the low 80s, high 20s centigrade. There is a very nice breeze and I wish I were sailing. What's the matter with that? You can also find good spots when you come to port in October. So, there are not so many tourists milling about. Do you really mind that? And many tourist places are closing down. So you go to the local's restaurants if you want to eat out. That's one solution, a good one.

And another one alternative, if it is July and August you must do it in. You choose an itinerary or two, that are out of harm's way, away from the Monster. There are so many islands besides the famous Cyclades that you can easily spend two lifetimes exploring.

The third solution I don't like, but it is another option. Go sailing somewhere else!

Back to the Cyclades for a minute. They are a group of fascinating islands indeed. Arid and treeless and greenless, in the very middle of the Aegean, they are known from antiquity, even before that! The legendary and cosmopolitan Myconos is one of them and so is the magical Santorini and the historical Delos. If it is them you want to see, take my advice. Avoid July and August. Go to the Saronic, the Sporades to the North, Eptanissa in the Ionian Sea to the West. There is almost endless groups of islands to see. Leave the Cyclades for the extremely hard core sailor who knows his boat and himself really well.

Boating and sailing in particular, are extremely popular in Greece and during the summer months, literally thousands of Europeans as well as others, descend on the Isles for a sailing adventure. The small ports, made to accommodate a few fishing caiques and a ferryboat at best, are neither equipped nor ready in any other way to receive the flotillas coming in daily. In Hydra,a wonderful island, I counted 124 masts on a dock that can comfortably take care of 20 to 30 boats.That was masts I counted. I didn't bother with the cabin cruisers! Hydra is lovely indeed. And picturesque and serene with no cars or mopeds roaming its quaint, narrow streets. One must be prepared to tie up to a sympathetic boat or two and jump over three or four others to step on dry land. And expect to find someone else tied up to you when you get back! In 9 out of 10 cases your anchor is either on top of somebody else's or theirs on top of yours. One suggestion here. Try to get to your destination by 2 to 3 o'clock in the afternoon. That's your best chance to get a spot on the quay. Most people like to sail, explore and come to port at 6 or 7 pm. By then it's too late for most ports, and they are jam packed with boats and there is a traffic jam of 5-6 boats looking for a spot simultaneously. So, at the end of the day when you're ready to relax, contemplate the events, decide what you want to eat, look for ice and water, it may well take a tremendous effort just to secure the boat. I've seen it thousands of times. 'Nough said. Remember the subtitle of this book was what NOT to do. You've been duly warned!

We got into sailing right away. I owe it to my non expert readers to familiarize them with some of the joys of sailing and what it is that creates this fascination, this mania if you wish, with it. The next chapter then, is going to attempt just that. Some of the necessary things to know about boats, sailboats, the sea, navigation, weather e.t.c. For those of you in the know, this is just a different slant.

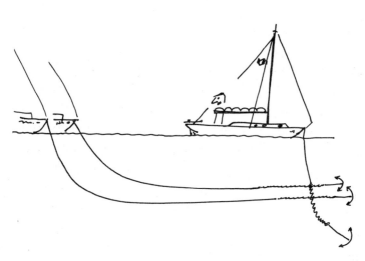

ANCHORING, MANEUVRE OR MANOEUVRE.

THE BOAT

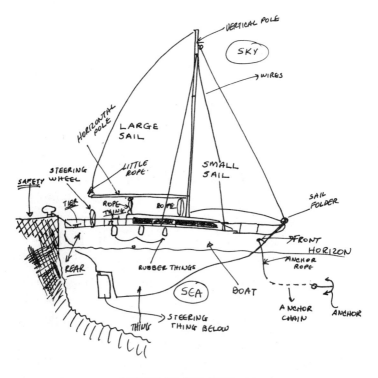

SAILBOAT AND ITS PARTS.

The boat is the most important part of your sailing experience outside of yourself, so we must spend a few pages on it. The little sketch I made for the preceding page just isn't enough. You may buy or charter your boat and there are many reputable companies in Greece that charter sailboats and many that aren't quite as reputable. Large companies charge large fees. That's been my experience. There are some good small operators at half the price, but that requires some digging. In a later section I list a couple whom I found to be dependable and reasonable, with good boats and equipment. If you wish to buy a boat, that's another chapter altogether, maybe even another book.

Charter boats are available in many sizes from 30 footers to 52 and of course the size you choose depends on how many people are in your party. The more the people, the bigger the boat. It makes sense. But also you must consider the experience of your crew. If worse comes to worse, hire a skipper as well. In which case you probably don't need this book either. Just don't try to learn how to sail on a bare boat charter in the summer in Greece. You'll either learn very quickly or you'll drown! And that's no way to start a sailing adventure. That's really sailing into your sunset.

The friends you pick to join you must really be friends and good ones at that. Otherwise ... good luck.

Back to the boat itself! As I was saying, the small diagram may not be enough, but it shows you a whole bunch of things you need to know in real terms, and not the pseudo-sophisticated terminology of the sailing crowd. That really complicates things because a rope is not really a rope but...imagine this it is a......sheet. Yes, of all things a rope becomes either a sheet or a line. Now, a line I can understand, but a sheet? Well it is a sheet if it controls a sail, and a line for everything else. Almost. You see now that my little diagram uncomplicates things and calls them by what they are.

Generally, a boat with one mast is a SLOOP, with two either a KETCH or a YAWL depending on where its steering is (before the 2nd mast a ketch, after a yawl, but not to worry) and very likely if it has three masts a SCHOONER, but it could be other things like a galleon, a brigadoon or an albania, because some of them are the size of Albania.

The sloop, which is the most common sailboat, has only one mast but two sails, a small one in front (jib)
and a large one (main) in the back. There is a very strange theory about how a boat is actually propelled by the wind force and it is not pushed but pulled, but I do think that somebody made it up just to complicate things and make them sound ...scientific so they could name a science after themselves and coin strange words like aerodynamics and

nautical. So I will not bother you with it or about any other sailing instructions. This is not a HOW-TO book but a HOW-NOT-TO, get it?

Suffice to say that you should NOT hoist up your sails while still in port. Motor your boat out of harm's way, point your bow (front) to the wind and raise your sails. Once under sail power, cut off your engine. Reverse the process when you come to port. Just to make sure a mile or so ahead of time, start your engine,point to the wind, lower your sails and secure them if you can, and get into port using your engine. Now if your engine doesn't want to start, I hope you are a damn good sailor, the wind is from the right direction and that you pray a lot. There are a couple of alternate solutions but I'll mention them in my...book for advanced or insane sailor techniques.

The above are just basic procedures as I said. What happens in between is the FUN.

Your charter boat should contain all you need for a comfortable, trouble free sail. My first one several years back even had some....Wayne Newton tapes. What else could I possibly want? Don't tell me Vivaldi because he hasn't made the top 40 here yet! Some of the amenities you can expect include a bathroom, irrationally called ''the head''. If you manage your size down to 3'6'' you'll also be able to take a shower in the very same space. You may have a small problem with your limbs and what to do with them as you try to wash the other parts of your body, but it is for such a short time, you should not let it ruin the rest of your trip. The larger, more comfortable (and more expensive) boats do not have a larger more comfortable head. They have two small ones!! It makes sense to me. Instead of having one person taking a nice comfortable shower, you can now have two people reducing themselves to half their normal size and taking two miserable showers simultaneously. Yes misery loves company even in nice and expensive sailboats. But they do have an advantage. In a totally mysterious way a water system circulates somehow through the engine and your shower water is anywhere from lukewarm to freezing. Smaller boats have only freezing water. To be fair, I speak with a Florida perspective, and to me any water below 90 degrees is freezing. To many of you accustomed to weather like what you get in Minnesota, Ohio, Sweden or Siberia, you might think of it as absolutely divine. It is all relative.

Besides the head, there is also a miniature kitchen called a galley for unknown reasons, which contains among other things, an energy consuming, battery operated (usually) refrigerator that keeps things luke....cool. If you want to have enough juice to start your engine, make sure you supplement your refrigerator with ice if and whenever it is available. Most stoves in the galley work, but few are ever used. They are kerosene operated and do a pretty fair job.

I never use mine except for coffee in the morning. I like salads, fruit and maybe a sandwich at noon and in the evening, if I am still hungry I enjoy a good local tavern, category C. If you really enjoy cooking, then go ahead and cook. Otherwise take my advice and don't. Eat out, it's good for the local economy and lets you concentrate on what this is all about, which is sailing. Now if you find yourself in a wonderful quiet cover, really away from it all and hungry at the same time, well then go ahead and fish and cook and live off of the sea!

Besides the galley and the head, you also have closets big enough for Liliputians and cots comfortable enough for Indian fakirs. You learn to live with both. First, you learn to live with a very basic wardrobe consisting of a bathing suit and a T-shirt that you wash once a week and you only wear on formal occasions. Secondly, your bed brings back memories and the nostalgia of the good old days in the army. Now, if you never went in the army, maybe your parents sent you camping once. Remember how much fun that was? Wouldn't you like to recapture those special moments of your youth? Did I hear you say yes, but in different ways? Well, this is sailing, an activity for the tough and hardy, for the nature lover, who tames the wind and endures the elements and survives 2 foot seas.

There you have it. Your dream boat. Now, however I must get technical and speak to you about some of the equipment and instruments that every boat should have, and how not to use it. The fun is over. This is serious stuff.

There are several instruments and organs actually too numerous to mention here, so I will give you an overview of what is absolutely necessary for navigation and safety. Most are user friendly if you've had some experience with them, but they could well become unfriendly under some situations, like when you are trying to figure out how in the world this life vest fits and the repeated 6 foot waves won't let you read the instructions! You better know ahead of time. So here is another "don't" for you . Don't wait till the last minute to locate some of these things.

In terms of importance in instruments, the compass is probably very important, maybe even more important than you think at first. The compass is divided in 360 little divisions called degrees in English and American alike. Most of the time it points to the North or at least at 0 which should also be 360. The compass helps you steer the course you like, if you know what it is. One or two words of caution. Do not put any large metal objects close to your compass or you may find yourself on an entirely different island than the one you had planned. If the compass spins madly, just think of how they must have navigated 2000 years ago in these very waters and long before the invention of the compass. And then pray a lot.

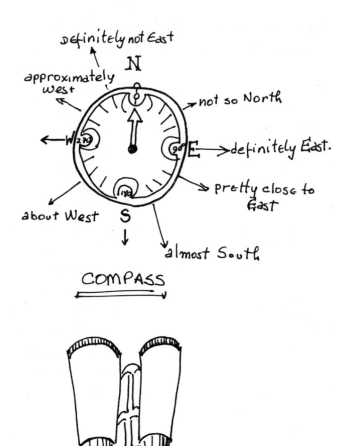

definitely not East

approximately
west

not so North

N

W 270

E

definitely East.

approximately west → W(270)

pretty close to
East

about West

almost South

S

COMPASS

BINOCULARS

Next to the most important instrument,
designed to look at beautiful specimens
of the opposite sex.

Another rather handy and fun at the same time thing, is the binoculars. The binoculars are very handy in bringing far away things close, for example interesting members of the opposite sex, who are innocently sunbathing at a distance too far to enjoy with the naked eye. You can also spot sailboat masts as you come close to a port, which is usually a good hint as to where you should be heading.

The VHF is a radio-like thing, with a small cord-attached mike, which has a button on it and which you must push when you want to talk, assuming of course that you've turned it on first. At the end of your statement make sure you say "over" or something that sounds like it, like "rover" or "roger" and then release the button so you can hear the other party.VHF has several channels, and the internationally used Ch.16 is fortunately also used here as well. Somehow the Greeks managed this one time to coordinate themselves with the rest of the world.That's quite reassuring actually. The VHF is a valuable instrument because with it you can actually communicate with other vessels and listen in on other people's conversations. Careful not to leave it on all night or your beer might be warm the next day if your battery goes down. The VHF has a channel selector, a volume control and a squelch button that allows you to constantly listen to static over the speaker. Some people like to have it on all the time,usually the cabin cruisers because they carry at least 200 batteries, to see what's happening around them.

Channel 16 is access to HELLAS RADIO and you can normally contact someone who in comically accented English will try to help you with info you may need. You can even ask them if and where you can find ice at a particular island. The only thing I noticed about the response, however, was that it came in Greek and it sounded less than gentle.

Another important instrument is the cassette tape player. It comes in very handy unless you are very interested in Greek talk shows or call-in programs, and they are the only things I've been able to get on the local radio once out at sea. Never any music. Not even Wayne Newton.

These then are the major instruments one really needs. It may be handy to have a log, which gives you your boat's speed, distance travelled and even time on some. This way you can calculate how far off course you really are.

Many boats also have a depth finder or sounder as well, which lets you know when you've hit bottom by emitting an irksome sound like a car alarm at a particular time when you don't want to hear anything at all, let alone a constant beeeeeeep.

Generally, all sailboats are equipped with a sail invetory that consists of some very exciting and exotic names like genoa, spinnaker, balboa and siamesc. They also have a number of ropes and winches and tackle and an engine somewhere as well as an inflatable dinghy. I could never figure out what the h is doing in dinghy since it is not pronounced. My dinghy was manufactured in Greece. It deflates itself automatically once the sun goes down, but promptly by 10am it's fine and ready to use again. Ingenious. I made it a point not to have a wreck after sundown!

I will not bore you with other minute details of everything on board. Most of you know it anyway and there are excellent reference books on the subject. Just make sure you have all the safety equipment, flares, harnesses-one per person- and all that and hope you never need them.

Of course, the alternative is that one can dispense with all that and take the....ferryboat. In which case the chapter on itineraries will be more interesting.

WEIGHING ANCHOR IN HYDRA & POROS & MYCONOS & SYROS & NAXOS & PAROS & SANTORINI e.t.c.

TYPES OF BOATS
IN THE GREEK SEAS

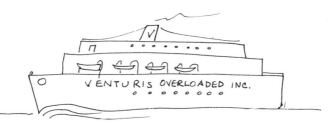

FERRY-BOATS CONTAINING USUALLY 6-8,000 TOURISTS 6-8,000 MOTORBIKES 4-6,000 AUTOS AND TRUCKS OF ASSORTED SIZES, VINTAGE 1920's.

CRUISE SHIPS VISITING MYCONOS & SANTORINI.

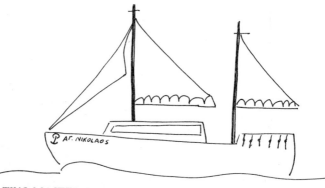

TWO MASTED SCHOONER LOOKING THINGS WHOSE SAILS HAVE SELDOM BEEN UNFURLED, FOR TOURISTS.

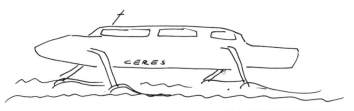

WEIRD LOOKING YELLOW & BLUE HYDROFOILS CALLED "DOLPHINS" TO GIVE AN UNDUE SENSE OF SECURITY.

INCREDIBLY LARGE TANKERS - FRFIGHTER AND WHO KNOWS WHAT ELSE MERCHANT MARINE SHIPS.

GREY, SLEEK LOOKING, NAVY VESSELS WITH OMINOUS WEAPONS ON THEM.

TYPES OF BOATS FOUND IN GREEK SEAS.

THE FUN BOAT (TAHÍ-PLO-O) SPEED BOAT.
THE DREAM BOAT OF MOST GREEK AUTO DRIVERS.

THE INFLATABLE TERROR.

THE MODEST FISHING ROW BOAT.

THA-LA-ME-GOS (THE NEAUVEAU - RIGHT STATUS SYMBOL)
IN VARIOUS SIZES FROM 30" ON TO OBSENE, BELONGING TO
SHIPPING MAGNETS ALSO OF VARIOUS SIZES, USUALLY
EQUIPPED WITH A SONY 27" T.V. AND FOREIGN CREW.)

FISHING CAIQUE (KA-EÉ-KEE)
USUALLY WHITE WITH BRIGHTLY COLORED TRIM.

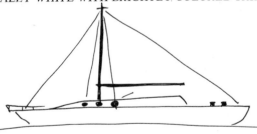

CHARTER SAIL BOAT, WITH OR WITHOUT A SKIPPER
CONTAINING 8-10 FRENCHMEN OR 4-6 ENGLISHMEN OR
GERMANS OR SWEDES OR DUTCH OR ITALIANS OR SWISS
GETTING THEIR ANCHORS TANGLED IN GREEK PORTS OF
CALL.

THE WEATHER

BEAUFORT SCALE

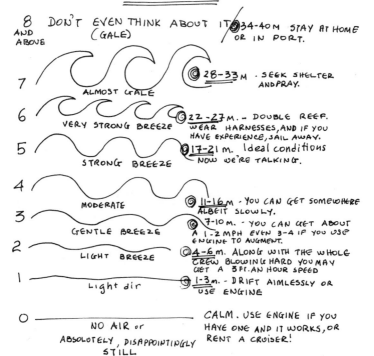

8 AND ABOVE — DON'T EVEN THINK ABOUT IT (GALE) — 34-40 M STAY AT HOME OR IN PORT.

7 ALMOST GALE — 28-33 M · SEEK SHELTER AND PRAY.

6 VERY STRONG BREEZE — 22-27 M. - DOUBLE REEF. WEAR HARNESSES, AND IF YOU HAVE EXPERIENCE, SAIL AWAY.

5 STRONG BREEZE — 17-21 m. Ideal conditions NOW WE'RE TALKING.

4 MODERATE — 11-16 M - YOU CAN GET SOMEWHERE ALBEIT SLOWLY.

3 GENTLE BREEZE — 7-10 M. - YOU CAN GET ABOUT A 1-2 MPH EVEN 3-4 IF YOU USE ENGINE TO AUGMENT.

2 LIGHT BREEZE — 4-6 m. ALONG WITH THE WHOLE CREW BLOWING HARD YOU MAY GET A 3 FT. AN HOUR SPEED

1 Light air — 1-3 m. - DRIFT AIMLESSLY OR USE ENGINE

0 NO AIR or ABSOLUTELY, DISAPPOINTINGLY STILL — CALM. USE ENGINE IF YOU HAVE ONE AND IT WORKS, OR RENT A CRUISER!

A very short chapter this one, mainly to give you a few more details about the monster MELTEMI, should you happen to meet up with it. Some of this info is folkloric, gathered by talking to old fishermen in the Cyclades, like captain Mitsos in Loutra on the wind swept island of Kythnos where predictably I tore my mainsail and I was only one of four boats that came in that day with torn sails. And most of these people were more experienced sailors than I. A small comfort that was, as we all had to wait it out about a week and then head to Syros where they have both the facilities and the knowhow to mend them properly if expensively. I didn't mind the layover. Some of the others did as they were on charter boats and limited time. I made a bunch of new friends, ate wonderful fresh, reasonably priced fish and lobster, and took a few hot baths in the local hot springs to boot. And to think that only by accident did I get there. Had it not been for the meltemi and the torn sail, I would have continued on to Syros and would have missed what turned out to be the surprise and the highlight of the summer, meltemi and all.

But I digress. Back to the meltemi. It is a Turkish word MELTEM which the Greeks adopted by adding an i at the end of it. It is as I said a July-August phenomenon frequently blowing itself into September albeit in a weakening form. It is a difficult wind because it is gusty and it creates unhumorous looking waves the size of the Grand Canyon. Not at all entertaining. Fortunately it is at its worst in the Central Aegean area, leaving other areas more navigable. There are 3-4 epecially difficult passes (BOURNAZI in the local sea lingo) that need to be mentioned as the winds there exceed the weather forecasts by 10-15 miles sometimes. One notorious such pass is CAVO DORO, from cape Sounion to KEA, or the other way around. It is only a bit more than 10 miles but they could seem more like 100! A real tough one at times.

The distance from MYCONOS or ANDROS to ICARIA called ICARIO PELAGOS is another dandy. And so is the one from MYCONOS to SYROS. A short one but a mean one. Up to Force 6 they are negotiable. Beyond that you had better know your boat really well and be on good terms with it. I stayed in port in Syros eight whole days before I dared to venture the 18 miles across with a daily Force 7-8-9 and a few gale warnings which prompted the local port authorities to disallow any vessels leaving port.

Usually the meltemi will slow down in the evening and stay down for the night. Usually, but not always. Around 6-7 PM the wind subsides and an hour or so later so do the waves. As the sun comes up it picks up strength and as it rises it gets worse. Fishermen told me that when the sun goes up so does the meltemi, when the sun goes down so does the meltemi. Another warning sign I was told is a long white cloud over an island. Well, I never saw a cloud all summer long, so I cannot tell you how true that tale is. The new moon is the tell tale and the forecaster for the month. If the new moon can't hold water, which means the crescent shape is vertical, then there 'll be no winds. If it is horizontal then watch out. I can't in all honesty say that that is very reliable either, matter of fact for quite some time I thought it was the other way around, and it didn't seem to make any difference.

Another local lore is about the dampness on your deck. If your deck is dry in the early morning it's best to stay put. Now, if it is dewy, it can mean little or no wind. I've always had some difficulty telling just how moist it's got to be before it gets to be dewy. When my deck in Florida in the summer is wet enough in the morning to actually wash it down with it, is that dewy enough? I've never seen it that dewy in Greece except in the winter and only when it rains.

So much for the local fishermen. But I will attest to the fact that moon or no moon, dew or no dew, Capt. Mitsos in Kythnos knew the weather better than the detailed 6:30 am Weather Bureau forecast did.

So, if you must get to your next destination 20 miles away or so, do it at 5:30 am or late afternoon if the forecast is for ugly weather. For myself, like the local fishermen, I prefer going into the day.

I mentioned briefly something about the Spiliades before. Careful. Do not come close to port with your sails up. I've seen several demasted boats because of the Spiliades. They are nastier in some places than in others, like the devastating Serifos, so best not to take any chances, drop your sails well ahead of time.

Seldom will you see any rain during the summer in Greece. Nor will you see too many clouds. This summer for example it did not rain any more than in the Sahara and now late October and still no rain. So even if you are stuck in port somewhere, you will always find a nice beach nearby and enjoy the day. Unless you'd rather stay aboard and polish brass.

Not much more to say on the weather. Was it Mark Twain that said that everyone is talking about the weather but no one is doing anything about it? Generally it is good April through October with the meltemi exception if you are sailing. And then again there is the IONIAN SEA to the west of Greece. And it has no meltemi. And it does have magical islands as well!

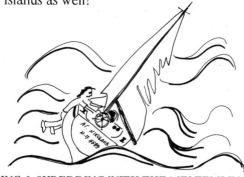

HEELING & SHREDDING WITH THE MELTEMI IN AUGUST.

THE   DON'Ts

We've already mentioned a few DON'Ts but there are so many that a whole chapter is necessary. We might also repeat some of the old don'ts, just to emphasize them, so if we make a mistake, we make it on the side of safety, as we sea people like to say. There are also a few Dont's that are peculiar to Greece and the Greeks. We learned the hard way!

* When you come to port and see a great, big beautiful open space at the dock, DO NOT even go close to it. It is reserved for ferryboats and-or Flying Dolphins. (See... diagram to identify) Not for you.

* Also DO NOT even think of getting close to fishing caiques. Those guys are very possessive of their property and anything that is within a few miles radius and if you happen to come across a mean one, watch out. They're not always wonderfully hospitable. A Stalone looking character, and about as intelligent as Rambo himself, dwells somewhere in Kythnos and seems to own all the public docks, even the side that says YACHTS. But it is written in English and it is doubtful that this guy can read anything let alone some sophisticated foreign language. Well avoid him. Unless, in his anger he starts throwing lobsters at you. They do have great lobsters in Kythnos!

* If you ever need help, make sure you negotiate the price beforehand. This is particularly true if you are out at sea. There are lots of folks out there, standing by their

VHFs with a view toward your boat. DO NOT throw them a line or catch theirs for either a tow or anything else, till all finances are taken care of, or they may own half of your boat by the time you come to port. And more. I did hear some veritable horror stories out there and thought I'd pass them along.

* DON"T argue with Greeks. You'll never win even if you are right. The only way to argue -and win sometimes- is to kill them with politeness. They are not used to it and they simply do not know how to respond to it. And at the end you might get what you want.

* Europeans in general are good seamen. So are professional Greeks, who may be good at seamanship but know little about rules and regulations that are not convenient for them. Stay out of the way of most Greek amateurs, particularly the loud ones. The less they know, the louder they get somehow. Be vigilant and watch their every move if they are docking next to you, to avoid any damages. If nothing else, it is entertaining.

* Always ask politely if you must tie up on somebody else's boat. Nobody ever refused me. Well, let me qualify it. No sailboater ever refused me. The cabin cruiser types, they are a different breed, aren't they?

* DO NOT neglect to instruct any visitors on your boat who are not boaters how to flush the head! Many an unpleasant hour has been spent by people I know and like, unclogging the thing.

*   Do not fire your 45 at the speed boat that just passed you 20ft away.

*   Do not find yourself in the unpleasant situation of being chased by a ferryboat. They are faster, a lot bigger and their wake uncomfortable for you. I swear that when the captains of those babies see you anywhere near their route, they come after you, if only to scare you. They did me. Fun and games. Stay out of their way by going out of yours. It's a lot safer. You see I know what I should do and I also know what they should do, and I am reasonably sure they know what they should do. The question is will they do it? Do not wait to find out if they are playing one sided sea chicken with you or not. Scram!!

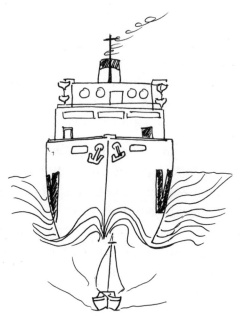

*   DO NOT get close to any speed boat whether it's standing still or not. They are being operated by the same drivers that have made Greece such a favorite with the demolition derby drivers around the world, and also by the demon driven motorcyclists of Athens. You know what I mean!

*   If you like to snorkel, do. Go ahead. If you like to scuba, don't. Because Greece as you may know is a very very old country, and there are many wrecks around that have been there for one, two or possibly even three thousand years. And those ancient boats possibly contain ancient treasures. Then again maybe not. Well you should not try to find out. That's the job of the government, which may take another 3000 years, but that's another story. So it (the gov't I mean) in its very finite wisdom, has specified the areas where scuba diving is allowed. Make sure you are in that area when you scuba. Now if you want to samba, that's another story too.

*   Which brings us to another DON'T. If you do come across any antiquities, Don't touch them, don't report them, don't do anything but scram again. You are supposed to report them, but if you do, the Greeks with their proverbial by now paranoia, may think you have something to do with the bands of ancient site robbers that go around and before things are cleared, the best part of your sailing adventure may have been spent in police department stations. Also do not buy any ancient looking things if you are interested in that sort of thing, unless they come from a reputable dealer with the appropriate papers.

* Do not go to Kalamaki or Zea or any marinas around Athens unless you absolutely have to. If you do, do not expect any courtesy, as they have so much business, they don't really need yours or mine, and besides they are civil servants with permanent jobs, avoiding work as best as they can. Also Kalamaki has a disco that on a normal Saturday night, but also on any night of the week in the summer, can be heard as far away as Scandinavia.

* Told you not to go close to fishing boats in port. Also DO NOT go close to them at sea, because they may be actually fishing, in which case most likely they have nets out, and you know what the nets can do to a propeller, don't you? It won't do wonders for the disposition of the fisherman either.

* If it's Santorini you 're looking for on your map, most likely you'll not find it. Do not despair. It also has another name: Thera or Thira depending on the map you have. This country is so old that sometimes I think that people just got tired of the same old names, got together and decided to change them. Some places may even have three names!! Then we have the problem of adapting them

to the Latin alphabet, and a bunch of more comical names come up. So you have CRETE and KRETE and KRITI and KRETA, also you'll find KERKYRA, KERKIRA, KORKYRA, and CORFU, or PIRAEUS, PIREAS, PIREEFS. Correspondingly they are the same places. But PAROS and POROS are not. Got to be careful with those things, you know.

*   And finally DO NOT, I repeat DO NOT dare leave port, without Rod Heikell's GREEK WATERS PILOT. It is an indispensible publication. It just doesn't just make your life a lot easier, it makes your life period. Trust me.

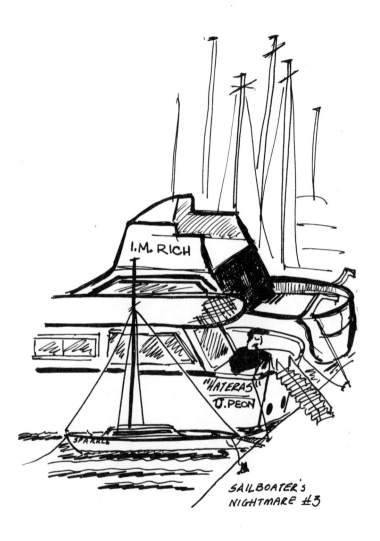

SAILBOATER'S
NIGHTMARE #3

THE ITINERARIES

There are 3000 islands, according to the last census. Or thereabouts. Even if one is to dismiss a thousand or so, given the propensity of the Greeks to exaggerate, there are still plenty of islands to visit, more than you can shake a stick at. Recent rumors have it that about 170 of them are inhabited by humans and also by Greeks. There are two limiting factors as I see it.

A- the direction of the winds and B- the amount of time you'll have available. Most people who charter, do so for two weeks. I'd make it three if you'll be going into meltemi weather and the Cyclades and if it is July or August.

The very first thing you'd want to do before you do anything else is to get your copy of the GREEK WATERS PILOT. Rod Heikell has divided his book into ten regions, very wisely so as they do make geographical sense. Then he goes on to explain, in formidable detail everything you need to know about every nook and crany. Which is wonderful because without his book I probably would have visited the disco at Kalamaki all summer long! Well maybe I would have gone to Aegina once or twice.

I can not say enough about Heikell's book He does everything so well and he misses no detail. But he gives you no itineraries. He lays the islands out for you with every minute and important detail, with all their coves and even the names of helpful tavern owners-part time yacht chandlers. Then it's your decision where to go. His is a factual, INDISPENSIBLE guide. This is my biased opinion, emotional at that, tinted with just a bit of logic, as to what and how much one can see in the course of two to three weeks, maybe even more. It still is your decision which group of islands to do. I can lay out enough itineraries here to last you for the next ten or even twenty years. And of course you've got to follow your own heart, in terms of what interests you. Do you want a historical itinerary? or one that's away from the crowds? or one that's into the cosmopolitan yacht-set? Do you want to be in a different port or cove every night, or do you like to stay a while if you find a spot you enjoy?

So you see the question of itineraries is almost too personal to answer logically and try to include a bit of everything in them. That's why I assume that Heikell said, here they are, go where you fancy the most.

Most chartered boats are in the marinas around Athens, which is a good point of departure -and return- for some itineraries, but not for others as it would take you most of your charter time just to get to your first island. There are now good reputable operators out of a number of islands so you can commence your adventure near the islands you want to visit. For instance if it is the Ionian Islands you want to see you can get started in Corfu or Lefkada, or if you want Dodecanissa, then Rhodos could be your starting point. Even if you insist on the Cyclades, Syros will be your point of departure. Again, don't get lost in your map looking for the Cyclades as they may well be spelled Kiklades, Cyklades, Kyclades or any reasonable or insane variation you could imagine! They are in the middle of the Aegean Sea or Aegeon Pelagos or Egeon or.......

Generally, I too have divided the Itineraries geographically, taking some advice from here and there, and from my own experiences, and those of others, and old fishermen, and charter boat skippers and,believe it or not, ferryboat captains. Yes indeed!

I do hope that in these routes you'll find what you're looking for, which is a tall order in two weeks. A little bit of everything perhaps, people when you want them, peace and serenity when you want it. Now if you're looking for a different port every night, that's not hard to do in Greece. If you are on the run, you can even do two ports a day! Suit yourselves. I am on the other side of the spectrum. I do not like the "If it's Monday it's got to be Mongolia" type of travelling, regardless of the means I'm using.I 'll go two miles or two hundred in one day. My decision to stop is mine. Do I like the place? Do I need to rest? Do I need time to regroup, to meditate, to empty the trash?

WEIGHING ANCHOR IN AG. MARINA, AEGINA.
(LORD KNOWS WHAT YOU CAN CATCH.)
(I'VE GOT A PHOTO TO PROVE IT!!)

U. PEON
NΠ 454Ξ

MOTOR BOATER'S DELIGHT

1.   **NORTHERN GREECE**

2.   **EASTERN EGEON (AEGEAN)**

3.   **SPORADES & EVIA**

4.   **DODECANNISSA**

5.   **KYKLADES (CYCLADES)**

6.   **SARONIKOS & EASTERN PELOPONISSOS**

7.   **KORINTHIAKOS & PATRAIKOS**

8.   **WESTERN PELOPONISSOS OR SOUTH IONION**

9.   **NORTHERN IONION**

10.   **KRITI (KRETE, CRETE etc)**

The order of the divisions is sort of arbitrary. I just started at the top and came around clockwise. I left Crete last as it is a beautiful and unique island, not to mention big, that demands three lifetimes, at least, on its own.

1. NORTHERN GREECE

If it is quiet and serenity you are seeking (most of the time) you've come to the right places. To begin with the scenery is entirely different from southern Greece. It's almost like being in another country, beautiful in its own way and majestic with sandy beaches and lots of trees and lots of greenery!! Not a very well travelled area by yachtsmen, it nevertheless has a lot to offer. To begin with, the Meltemi is very mild here, a Force 3-4 much of the time makes life bearable if not extremely exciting. Then the gulfs in HALKIDIKI with the clear waters and magnificent densely wooded countryside, the changes between mountains and shores, make the area magical and fascinating. The third peninsula is Mt.Athos with some 10 monasteries on the 6500 ft mountain. This is to Greeks what Lhasa is to Tibetans. Only be careful. Women are not allowed on it or in the sea that surrounds it for at least 500 meters from the shore.

Besides Halkidiki, there are two if not three islands that are green and hospitable and unspoiled and beautiful and accesible:THASSOS and SAMOTHRAKI and a third that, depending on your time, you could get to but geographically it belongs elsewhere, LIMNOS. You can do it this time around or next time from a different approach.

For this area, a two week charter, if not longer, starting in THESSALONIKI is advisable, then heading first South and then East towards the gulfs, the islands or the cities KAVALA and ALEXANDROUPOLIS.

2.   EASTERN EGEON

If MITILINI or LESVOS (same island. Remember our game in the first chapter?) is not the jewel of the Greek seas, not to exaggerate and say of the whole Mediterranean, then I don't know what is. And HIOS to the south. And from there you can get to the "cosmopolitans" south of HIOS to SAMOS or the quiet places and LIMNOS to the north.

MITILINI is a large island a bit out of the way but well worth it once you get there. You can spend the whole summer in MITILINI on its beaches. Its mountains, its bays, its fishing villages and hospitable islanders. Here you will not find the fancy, sophisticated crowds seeking the latest discos, but you will find some wonderful tavernas with excellent food and reasonable prices and friendly innkeepers. And that's what I am looking for, as I am tired of the "finesse" of other well travelled places with the token donkey to verify its authenticity. HIOS is the same and there are several smaller islands around that are small gems as well.

The weather here is a bit stiffer than in Northern Greece in the summer and the meltemi monster will blow a consistant Force 4-6 and sometimes more.

You could spend two weeks easily in this area and still want more.The current difficulty is chartering from any place that is close enough without having a two day trip to get there.

3.   SPORADES AND EVIA

If you start from Athens, the most travelled and safest route is the one between EVIA (or EBOIA, EUBOEA, EVOIA etc) and the mainland because it has a number of small ports and it is not as open to the Meltemi as is the route out in the open Egeo with few shelters on the eastern side of EVIA. Care must be taken when in HALKIS. It's one of the few places in Greece where you have to put up with tides of any sort. At HALKIS the flow changes every six hours. It's pretty strong so it is best to go with it . There is also a bridge with temperamental operators not world famous for their hospitality.

Once through, you should have no difficulty reaching VOLOS, although I would not consider it a prime destination. There are a whole bunch of other little places I'd prefer to see and I'd go more on the wind, sailing and the time of the day. Care should be taken also if the meltemi outside is Force 5-7. You may get some Spiliades (remember them?) off of the mountains and some currents in the narrows.

SKIATHOS, SKOPELOS, ALONISOS, the Sporades, and a few more little islets and the lonely SKIROS are a treat the moment you are past the TRIKERI peninsula. The meltemi is here N,NNE, but not the vicious southern type. Apparently it hasn't picked up speed yet. The area has quite a few sailing craft because it could well be the best sailing in Greece. The islands are green with beautiful sandy beaches and several anchorages that are both safe and picturesque. Quite touristy, SKIATHOS is the closest of the SPORADES and it has the reputation of having the best beach in the Egeon, Koukounaries, which is not a tongue twister, even in Greek.

SKOPELOS and ALONISOS are small but very very green and prosperous, with a number of small islets with good anchorages, such as NISOS PERISTERI, and NISOS PELAGOS.

Somewhat out of the way is SKIROS or Skyros, take your

pick. It is the largest of the Sporades. Skiros reminds one of the KIKLADES or at least part of it does as the northern part of the island is fertile and cultivated. The south with wonderful wild scenery is a good introduction to what one will get in the KIKLADES. Because of the lonely aspect of SKYROS and the winds,(it is wide open to them) and a distance from the other islands it is not as touristy a place, and its people to date still retain the old world honest charm not the plastic variety that comes with the hordes of foreigners.

The Eastern side of EVIA I would not recommend. With KIMI the only port and a few safe anchorages, and the direct exposure to a strengthening Meltemi the more south you travel, and the wind constantly behind you, it makes it difficult to enjoy its rugged, wild beauty, unless it's not Meltemi time.

4.   **DODECANISSA**

Although the word means twelve islands, there are several more than twelve either because somebody could not count and went unchallenged or because of strange, mysterious and medieval reasons. The best way to sail them is to book directly from RODOS, RHODOS, RHODES etc and not spend much time doing the rest of the Egeon first. Unless you have plenty of time (4 weeks or more) and want to do the whole lot or as much as possible.

The Meltemi is here as well, blowing mostly NW-W with a constant Force 4-6 maybe 7. It's almost a daily routine. That's in the summer. Spring and fall are the good times with a Southeasterly 2-5. Again here we have swirling, twirling winds on the lee side of the islands in the summer. Use caution and reef your sails even on a mild force 5 just to be on the safe side and close to KALYMNOS, KOS, PATMOS or TILOS.

A good voyage will take you from RODOS to SIMI, TILOS, NISSIROS, KOS, KALYMNOS, LEROS, PATMOS, SAMOS and IKARIA if you have the time, and if the winds have been fair with you, you can start your Southern descent stopping at LEVITHA, ASTIPALEA, back to Nissiros, Simi and RHODOS.
We've left the lonely KARPATHOS and KASSOS to the SW of Rodos but they could be part of another itinerary going toward KRETE, some other time. You just can't see all 3000 islands the first time around!

RODOS is the most popular of all the Greek islands with millions of tourists each year. Its climate is hot in the summer but temperate in the winter and a favorite from ancient times of kings and queens, and Romans and Venetians and Genoese and knights and Pashas and the Italians again till 1947 when she came home to mother Greece, finally. A good spot to start your adventure and to finish it. Rodos is very cosmopolitan and sophisticated with just cause. She is beautiful! When you have had enough of the touristy thing, you head north to tiny SIMI away from the noise and the traffic. Simi is laid back quiet with well protected anchorages and main port. Now the quietest of all may well be TILOS just SE of Simi. And lovely too.

Or go to NISSIROS due W from Simi NW from Tilos Nissiros is a volcanic island with rich soil cultivated by the locals. This too is a quiet place, not touristy at all with very friendly and genuinely warm inhabitants. Heading north to KOS, you come into tourist territory again. And I do mean tourist, with discos one on top of the other. This is where Hippocrates lived in ancient times. North to Kalymnos on the way to LEROS. If you stop in Kalymnos, the sponge capital of Greece I would recommend VATHI. Leros is lovely reasonably peaceful with good vegetation and flowers. NE to PATMOS and you've completed another two week itinerary. Now all you have to do is return the boat to RODOS.

5.   KIKLADES

This is windy country!! I do not recommend it for July or August. I told you all about it before. No sense in wasting pages. Yet, there will be those of you that are at this very moment reading this as you are stranded somewhere in a Kikladic port waiting the wind to die down. Remember, I gave you alternatives!

You could get started from Athens but if it is the KIKLADES you want why not get started from SYROS? Regardless, SYROS is a great island to visit, particularly Ano Syros where at the height of the tourist season you might find two more tourists but I wouldn't make a bet.

If you do get started from Athens the first stop I would suggest is KYTHNOS and especially Loutra on the East side. Not only is it a logical spot, but a wonderful one at that, and to imagine that I came upon it by sheer.....accident. Namely torn mainsail. Loutra is a small fishing village its only tourists being the yachtsmen that come in away from the meltemi if barely so. Also some visitors to the therapeutic hot springs. When in Loutra see Takis the owner operator of the... Yacht Club. Takis will get you free hot showers, free water, wonderful fish, the latest weather forecast for the area, you name it, he'll do it. Also, see if you can find my friend Capt. Dimitri Sourlis, a repatriate Greek from the U.S. with a nack for catching

lobster. Say hi to him from me. God bless him. And ol'
Capt.Mitsos the best weather forecaster in all the Egeon
Pelagos.

Next I'd go to Syros. Dock on Finika and take the bus to
Ermoupolis, the main port, which is large but you could
not get a good night's sleep for all the tea in China or olive
oil in Greece. And see Ano Syros. From SYROS you have
a number of choices. (A) Across to MYCONOS, then to
TINOS , ANDROS, KARYSTOS in South EVIA, KEA
and back to Athens, or south (B) to PAROS (I prefer
ANTIPAROS), before that you could do MYKONOS if
everyone insists, NAXOS, IOS where you can leave your
boat for a day or two and take the ferry to SANTORINI. I
can't in all honesty recommend that you sail to
SANTORINI because once there, there is virtually no
place to anchor and definitely no place to dock that's not
wide open to the seas. But I would be amiss in not telling
you to go to SANTORINI or THIRA. She is the most
unique, wonderful, magical, mystical island of them all.The
IOS solution is the best for the sailors. From IOS you have
a number of alternatives. I' d prefer SIFNOS or if you
have time and fair winds SIKINOS, FOLEGANDROS and
then SIFNOS . Should you go to SERIFOS watch out for
the Spiliades, they are monstrous there. From there you
can easily return to SYROS, if that was your port of
departure or head NE to KYTHNOS, KEA and back to
the jungle in KALAMAKI. Sounion was a nice anchorage,
till it burned down this year.

6. SARONIKOS & EASTERN PELOPONISSOS

The KIKLADES will require a very minimum two weeks not to say three. SARONIKOS is a good choice for those that can only do a week, and still a good choice to stay out of the Meltemi monster for two weeks if you head into ARGOLIKOS and NAFPLIO and somewhat south, if time permits.

EGINA or AEGINA is your first port. It has wonderful pistachio nuts here, the harbor is safe if very busy, it's so very close to Athens you see. There are a couple of nice anchorages, one in AYIA MARINA on the east side and another behind ANGISTRI right across from EGINA at a spot called LIMENARIO.

WEDNESDAY: WASH DAY

From Egina down into POROS or you could go SW to EPIDAVROS and take a side trip to the nearby famous ancient theater. POROS has two or three very good and very protected anchorages as well as a picturesque if touristy port. Careful going through the channels.

The next natural stop is HYDRA or IDHRA. Sometimes I swear they just don't know exactly where to put that h. HYDRA is a scenic, historic island with, thank goodness, no MOTORS of any kind on it! Unfortunately it has a lot of tourists and some of them are the two hour variety. Oh well, it's a colorful if absolutely dry island with only its main port to dock. Get there early if you must!

SPETSE or SPETSAI is the next stop although there are a couple of islets where one can anchor and take a dip, such as DOKOS and TRIKERI and then go to SPETSE which is a touristy island as well. Just writing this I had an idea to rate the islands according to their tourist numbers. For me and most of the people I've come in contact with while sailing, it is the non-tourist traps that trap us. Maybe in the next edition I will have somthing like a reverse star rating system such as HYDRA * or KIPARISSI**** because it has very few tourists. Across from SPETSE is a delightful bay called PORTO HELI that makes for a good anchorage with plenty of dock spaces as well and a very safe place it is. That's for those of you going beyond the one week and into the second. There are a number of other locations across the coast, TOLOS perhaps having the best sandy beach in the area.

From there you move on to NAFPLIO, a fascinating town with a medieval fortress, plenty of good docking, good fish taverns and for what it offers, relatively few tourists. Taking the PELOPONISSIAN coast south, you'll come across ASTROS. one of my favorite villages SAMBATIKI, LEONIDION, KIPARISSI, YERAKA, and the mystical medieval town on the island MONEMVASIA. If you dare go and have the time tosail that far south it is well worth the effort.

7.   KORINTHIAKOS & PATRAIKOS KOLPOS

I never thought of this long body of water as a destination in itself but rather as a passage from the easten side to the western or vice-versa. But a destination it is as it does have great areas that one should not just pass up on their way through. From east to west, or even the other way around it is good to go the long way at least once, the 150 mile voyage to south Peloponissos and around it. There are some noteworthy islands to the south of PELOPONISSOS, KYTHIRA, ANTIKYTHIRA and ELAFONISSOS some good ports like METHONI and KORONI and some great beaches. The next pass however has got to be through the Korinth Canal expensive as it might be. Either before it or after it you have the long Gulf, some 60 miles long having two names PATRAIKOS close to the city of PATRAS to the west and KORINTHIAKOS to the east close to the city of KORINTH. It makes sense.

Before you get to the east side of the canal coming from Athens, or after going through the canal west to east, the area of ELEFSIS and its bay is industrial with all that goes with it anywhere in the world but worse here. Try to go through it as quickly as you can unless of course you have a keen interest in boats, oil refineries, cement plants and so forth.

Here, not knowing your direction and it could well be either, I will start east to west. You reverse it if you are coming from the IONION PELAGOS.

The weather is erratic in the whole lake like gulf as it is affected both from the Egeon and the Ionion winds and in areas they sort of funnel through. But there are wonderful coves and bays and out of the weather places, even small islets that are not too far away as the gulf is quite narrow.

One can easily zig-zag across from the PELOPONISSOS to the mainland and spend the best part of ten years doing it. KIATO may well be your first stop. It is a busy town has a decent little port and wonderful beaches nearby such as XYLOKASTRO. Or if you want some rest after the 3.2 mile trip through the canal you could anchor off of Loutraki, a hot bath resort favored by those of us who have reached that certain age which requires the warm lubrication of our joints.

ITEA and GALAXIDI, the latter being another favorite of mine, could be your next stops. Galaxidi is a quiet village well preserved, clean with very few modern buildings. It is also an access to Delphi which could be reached by taxi.

NISSIS TRIZONIA and NAFPACTOS after that with its almost perfectly preserved medieval port-fortress are a couple more musts here before going to PATRAS.

8. WEST PELOPONISSOS, SOUTH IONION

Perhaps I confused you. Forgive me. It is both the IONION and the IONIAN. PELAGOS which is one of the Greek words for sea takes IONION before it. THE IONIAN is followed by SEA, in English. Simple isn't it?

Well, if one starts one's voyage from the IONIAN island of LEFKADA or from PATRAS, one has a couple or three choices from which to pick. See, I did not finish my sentence with a preposition! One choice is the northern Islands and another is the southern Islands and a third choice yet, is the south and western side of PELOPONISSOS. An interesting two week or longer itinerary may be made up, even though you'd be going down the coast and then coming up the coast, by alternative ports and anchorages so you would not visit the same place twice unless you wanted to. Of course if time is of no issue and you decide to do the complete circle of PELOPONISSOS then you'd have no such problem.

The west side of Peloponissos is rugged with precipitous mountains next to the coast and some great beaches. Loutra Killinis across from Zakynthos is one of the finest sandy beaches of the Mediterranean and that includes the Riviera. South to KATAKOLON. From here you can if you wish, visit ancient Olympia some 25 miles away by taxi or bus from nearby Pyrgos. It is worthwhile even if antiquities is not your thing and you've seen too many ruins by now.

From KATAKOLON and about thirty miles south, a nice sail with fair winds is KIPARISSIA. Great beaches but not a great harbor. What can you do, you can't have it all. If the weather is not too fierce, you can anchor here, or move on to NISSIS PROTI or MARATHOUPOLIS or better yet PILOS or PYLOS or NAVARINO or.... I forget. PILOS is fairly well protected and has an adequate harbor. The town is attractive and worth a visit.

Just 5 miles to the south there is METHONI another favorite of mine. Are you tired of listening to that by now? Well, I haven't been any place I haven't liked. But some I like more than others, and this is one of them. Methoni's got it all, medieval fort, good fish, few tourists, no discos, quaint village streets, nice sandy beach and is very close to KORONI which I also like and PETALIDI, and on a larger scale deep inside MESSINIAKOS the town of KALAMATA with its world renowned olives, and coming around the gulf we find LIMENI a charming village in a unique setting with little or no tourism, as yet. On to MEZAPO a fishing harbor in an imposing setting and I am running fast out of superlatives and save one gulf we've almost come around. Is it worth going back or continuing through to the Egeon and through the canal? You the winds and your time decide!

9. EPTANISSA - THE IONIAN ISLANDS AND THE WEST COAST

EPTANISSA means the seven islands. I counted more than seven but then again perhaps I am not such a good mathematician. Who am I to argue with the descendents of Pythagoras and Euclid?

Whole books have been written about CORFU, KERKYRA alone and Lawrence Durrell sang her praises. How can I possibly add anything else? The only thing I 'll mention is that you can spend a lifetime there let alone visit it on a sailing trip. Yet CORFU is just one of the seven? beautiful Ionian islands. Just south of Corfu is PAXI and the smaller sister ANTIPAXI. I've spent some time there and I have been enchanted by its beauty and I always long to return. Lakka, a natural bay away from any wind with great tavernas, Longos, a small fishing village, Mongonissi a great sandy beach, and Gaios, the main port one of the most picturesque and underrated spots. Thank goodness.

Across to the Mainland there is PARGA. Do not miss it. It is another one of those favorite although touristy places. How could it not be? How could it not have been discovered? PARGA has it all as well, including a Norman castle and a couple of treed islets with white churches and good fish and out of the way discos and sandy beaches and.... shall I go on?

LEFKAS or LEFKADA is an island by virtue of a man made canal but it has marvelous satellite islets including one you cannot go to, Scorpios, because it belongs to the estate of Aristotle Onassis. Right across from it though is MEGANISSI which is nicer anyway. The east coast of LEFKAS is great and protected. NIDRI, SPARTO-HORI,VLIHO, SIVOTA, POROS and VASILIKI to the south end are all good spots.

Across to the mainland there is KALAMOS and MITICAS and then south to ITHAKI or ITHACA, Odysseus island. Here the MUSTS are FRIKES and VATHI. Good anchorage at AETOS.

Directly to the west and a very short distance away is KEFALONIA , KEPHALINIA, CEPHALONIA or...... another magnificent island with post card quality harbors and beaches. FISKARDO and ASSOS are indeed frequently featured in post cards you see all over Greece. MYRTOS and LOURDAS are two of the finest beaches anywhere on this planet, including the famous Big Sur in California.

The last stop on this tour is ZAKYNTHOS or ZANTE. The town itself although demolished by an earthquake in 1953, has grown again perhaps not as in its earlier glory but still pleasant and in a nice setting with the hills above her. LAGANA and KERI on the south side. The west side of Zante is spectacular sheer limestone cliffs and caves and crystal aqua waters.

10.   CRETE, KRITI

Inhabited since the Neolithic times CRETE is the largest of the Greek islands and a very important one it is. I've left it last because it is not the kind of an island that you make two or three stops at and seen most of it. It merits a tour of its own. Going with the wind which in the summer is NW and sometimes more of a westerly than anything else, it matters not which route you take around it. My preference would be east to west and I'd start and finish in HANIA. There are many great coves and bays and gulfs and harbors and resorts on CRETE on the North as well as on the South coasts. And in such a variety as to please every taste.

HANIA itself is a treat. The old city around the harbor is fascinating in its mixture of periods and architectures. Venetian and Turkish and modern all together in a strange harmony, embracing and welcoming the visitor. Touristy it is but happily so, unlike IRAKLION which I'd recommend you 'd give it a miss if it weren't for the palace of KNOSSOS just 2.5 miles from city center. And the museum in the city. Knossos was built around 1700 BC, that's some 3700 years ago and it was excavated in the beginning of this century. With statistics like that even the most disinterested person could not turn a deaf ear.

In between HANIA and IRACLIO is the lovely town of RETHYMNO with its small old and charming (I really mean it, I was indeed charmed) Venetian harbor. The SPINALONGA lagoon is worth a visit before coming to AGIOS NIKOLAOS. Spinalonga island abandoned, looks and feels haunted. You see it was a leper colony for many years, a long time ago. The colony was right below the

Venetian fort. Ag. Nikolaos was a fishing village. It no longer is. Today it is a RESORT with capital letters as you can see. Nearby ELOUNDA may well be the most expensive Greek resort. It may be fit for kings and prime ministers and presidents but it ain't for me.

Next stop : SITIA a very pleasant surprise, I prefer it 1000 times to Elounda, but that's my taste. I also loved SIDEROS right before turning south. It is rugged, isolated and unfriendly and eerie but very, very quiet.

IERAPETRA could be a nice spot, at least so think the thousands of tourists that come to its many many hotels. But then again there is GAIDURONISSO, much nicer and KATO ZACROS a beautiful sandy beach, KALI LIMENES, MATALA, AGIA GALINI, SFAKIA, LIMNI and the very picturesque LOUTRO and the again touristy PALEOHORA before you turn north and head for KISSAMOS and back to HANIA. Two weeks may not be enough for Crete. You always seem to discover something that's not in any book. It's an island full of surprises.

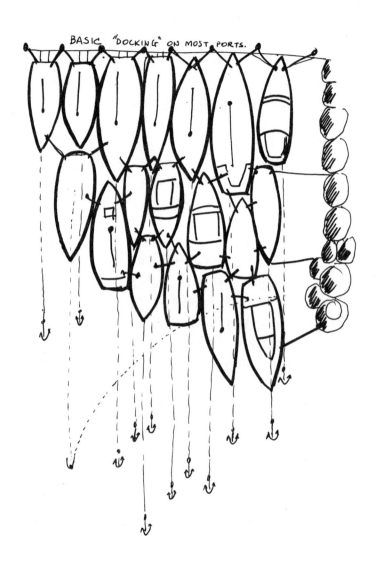

BASIC "DOCKING" ON MOST PORTS.

NAVIGATION
HELPFUL THINGS
AND MORE

1.   NAVIGATION

We've come this far, we've spoken about so many things and not a word about Navigation. Shame. This is the catch-all chapter. Navigation, indices, tables appendices, you name it and everything else we may have forgotten.

Much has been said about navigation, mostly by navigators. Navigation is very simple indeed even unnecessary in Greece, because even if you know not what you are doing you are bound to hit land, sooner or later. Most navigation is by dead reckoning. I just don't like the first part of this phrase. Let me explain what dead reckoning means. It really means a rough estimate of where you want to go by looking at the.....sun. It was the method used long before the sextant was invented. No statistics are available from that period, but that first word could not have come about strictly by accident.

The very first thing one needs in order to navigate is a map and secondly a destination. The Admiralty maps as old as they are, still are your most reliable source to tell you exactly where you are. Now you also need a ruler which is pretty straight. Most boats come equipped with a strange looking contraption that has two straight edges attached in such a way as to almost always remain parallel. Every Admiralty map also has two or three compasses-remember the sketch? Well these are actually printed on the map. Now the process is very simple. First you ask anyone who is walking around aimlessly on the dock admiring the boats, to tell you where it is that you are after all. Once this is known with some certainty, then you proceed to locate your position on the map. As soon as that is accomplished you must decide where it is you want to go and whether that place is anywhere on the map you have in front of you. Now if amidstream you decide to sail the lake Maracaibo and you are in Greece, well good luck. Having returned to normalcy, you locate your destination, you position the contraption so that it connects the two, where you are and where you want to go, and you "walk " it gently, so it does not slide too far out of parallel, to the compass so that the straight edge goes right through the center of it. There you have it! You are now a navigator! You have right in front of you on that compass the reading in degrees you want. Careful that you read it in the direction you need to go and not the opposite or you'll end up in an entirely different island again.

Now if you are sailing aimlessly just for the joy of sailing, I have another suggestion for you. Listen to the weather forecast. Next go to your map and see what islands are in the most favorable location for the wind direction forecast and ...sail there. Not a bad idea. I've done it successfully several times.

See how easy navigation really is if it is explained to you properly? Now if you want to know distance as well, find the dividers, they must be somewhere close to where you found the maps. The time has come to see what those babies are for. You open them up from where you are to where you want to go and then to the lines on the sides of the map with those funny little lines. Well each one of them is a mile and there PRESTO you have your distance as well!

There are a few other things to consider such as magnetic north and true north, variations, tides, currents etc but fortunately Greece suffers very little of any of these. Oh, there are a few reefs below the surface, there is the unexpected BURINI in the fall and a few other perils but why should we dwell on the negative? Let's go on to other things. O.K.?

2. HANDY WORDS TO RECOGNISE

AGIOS, AGIA, AYIOS, AGHIO	=SAINT
AKROTIRI	= CAPE
ANATOLI	= EAST
ARODO	=ANCHOR OUT
DITIKA	=WESTERLY
FAROS	=LIGHTHOUSE
IFALOS	=REEF
KAVOS	=CAPE
KOLPOS	= GULF
LIMANI	=HARBOR
LIMENARHIO	=PORT POLICE
MITI	=CAPE
MOLOS	=BREAKWATER
NERO	=WATER
NISI,NISIS,NISOS	=ISLAND
NOTIOS	=SOUTHERN
ORMOS	=BAY
PELAGOS	=SEA
PORTO	= SMALL HARBOR
REVMA	=CURRENT
SCALA	=STAIRWAY,QUAY
SCINI	=ROPE, LINE
SCOPELOS	=REEF
STENO	=STRAIT
TELONIO	=CUSTOMS
VATHI	=DEEP
VORIOS	=NORTHERN
VRAHOS	=ROCK, REEF

3. - THE WINDS

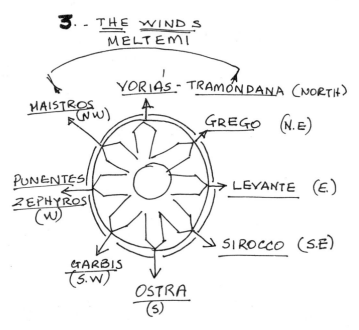

MELTEMI

YORIAS - TRAMONDANA (NORTH)

MAISTROS (NW)

GREGO (N.E)

PUNENTES ZEPHYROS (W)

LEVANTE (E.)

SIROCCO (S.E)

GARBIS (S.W)

OSTRA (S)

GREEK NAMES FOR THE WINDS

VORIAS — NORTHERN
ANATOLIKOS — EASTERN
NOTIAS — SOUTHERN
DITIKOS — WESTERN

4.   A BIT OF HISTORY

As I mentioned time and again, Greece is a very, very old country. I mean very old. So, as a result she has an awful lot of HISTORY, so much of it that in fact the Greeks had to invent a word for it and "History", a greek word, came into being. It is natural in all those years of history to have one's good moments and bad moments, ups and downs so to speak. The poor Greeks were at first threatened by the Persians or Medes then by themselves then the Romans actually came into Greece for 350 years or so, then the Ostrogoths invaded and devastated Greece. Once they were done and a few years later the Slavs did the same thing and the Bulgars and the Franks and the Turks and the Venetians. The Brits and the Italians took "care" of some Greek areas for a period of time in more recent years and then of course the Germans during World War II. Throughout all this, roughly 6000 years of it the Greeks have also been fighting themselves mostly in politics but also in combat. Battered but never really beaten, somehow they recover and continue to fight one another.

Few of Greece's visitors have had the benefit of a classical education, not unlike the Greeks themselves. When looking at some ruins, and in Greece it is unavoidable, the visitor does not quite know if something is Prehistoric or it belongs in the 19th century, like the buses in Athens. This little chart then is for your quick reference and information. It is not perfect, it is something like Instant-History, the fast food and digestion variety. Perhaps it can help put some order in what may well be a chaotic chronological disorganization in your head and answer things that you were afraid to ask, lest you be considered an utter idiot.

SOME LANDMARKS

4500BC-2000BC	Prehistory-Cycladic era
2000-1450	Minoan-Crete, Knossos
1500-1100	Mycenean
1200-700	Archaic era
	Homer,Olympics
700-350	Athens and Sparta
477-387	Classical period
	Parthenon, Socrates
	first plays
356-221	Macedonian era
200-BC-330 AD	Roman rule
324 AD-14th cen	Byzantine Empire
1200AD-1550 AD	Franks & Venetians
1453-1830	Turkish occupation
1831	Modern Greek Nation
World War I	Joins Western allies
World War II	With Western alliance
1941-44	Occupied by Germans
1967-74	Military Junta
1981	Greece joins European Common Market

5.   USEFUL NUMBERS

VHF	CH	16
HELLAS RADIO General Info.	CH	86
WEATHER Close to Athens	CH	8

Local fishermen
if you understand Greek

RADIO AM 70.0   At 6:30am daily detailed weather
                            forecast Greek and ENGLISH

National Weather Service   01 969 9306

CHARTERING

YACHT OWNERS ASSO.	452-6335 PIREAS
GREEK YACHT BROKERS	323-0330 ATHENS
SPYROS CARAYANNIS	417-2902
MAISTRALI -SYROS	(0281) 23-742
Cyclades charters FAX	(0281) 22-478 Makis
Capt. Mihalis	202-4774

PUBLICATIONS besides Admiralty maps

GREEK WATERS PILOT by Rod Heikell
IMRAY, LAURIE, NORIE & WILSON LTD
ENGLAND (O480) 62114
The only book you'll need. The Bible so to speak.
If you want more, go ahead spend your money.
But don't leave home without ROD!

6.   THE ODYSSEY

The very first epic about sea and sailing adventures, by Homer, of unknown surname, written about 800BC-750BC. The hero Odysseus, Ulysses if you prefer and his 10 year saga of trying to return home after the war in Troy. Now, I have some of my own theories as to why it took him so long. For one, he spent some 7 of those years on Calypso's Island.(She was gorgeous). For another, he was blown by an apparently strong Meltemi from Sounion all the way to Africa, past Crete and all. Remember what I was telling you about the Monster Meltemi? Well, here's ancient proof! Besides in those days they relied on Dead Reckoning for navigation! Here's some of Odysseus's stops, so you can associate them with whatever it is that you are planning.

- 1 TROY
- 2.MARONIA,NORTHERN GREECE*
-3.SKYROS, SPORADES*
-4.MALEA, PELOPONISSOS*
-5.LIBYA
-6.PALEOHORA, CRETE*
-7.GRAMBOOSA, CRETE*
-8.MEZAPO, PELOPONISSOS*
-9.PAXI, IONION*
-10.NEAR PARGA, MAINLAND*
-11.LEFKADA, IONION*
-12.MALTA
-13.CORFU, IONION*
-14.ITHACA, IONION*

A MODEST MAP IS PROVIDED HEREIN OF ODYSSEUS'S ODYSSEY.

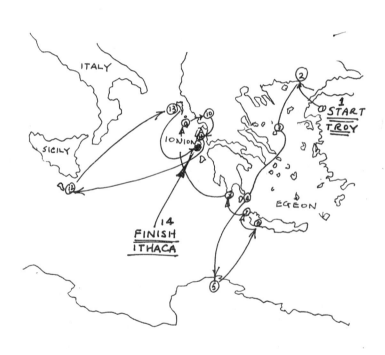

7 NAUGHTY KNOTS

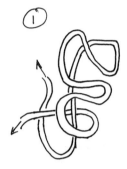

THE NIGHTMARE KNOT

IMPOSSIBLE TO TIE.
FREQUENTLY CALLED
UPON TO UNTIE.

THE ESS KNOT

A GOOD BEGINNER'S KNOT
DESIGNED TO UNTIE EASILY
MATTER OF FACT WITHOUT
EVEN TRYING.

THE UNKNOT - KNOT.

IT LOOKS AS THOUGH YOU
KNOW WHAT YOU ARE DOING.
BUT NOT REALLY.

THE GREEK KNOT

IMPOSSIBLE TO TIE OR UNTIE
A SURE BET TO SECURE
ANYTHING TO ANYTHING
FOREVER.

THE GORDIAN KNOT

OH WELL YOU KNOW
WHAT HAPPENED TO
THIS ONE.

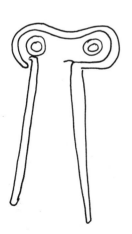

THE ATHENIAN KNOT

SIMPLE & ELEGANT
BUT OF LITTLE USE.

ABOUT THE AUTHOR

Vernon is basically a non-bourgeois kind of a guy, trapped some of the time in doing bourgeois kinds of things, much to his chagrin. Having raised three sane sons two of whom are card carrying, paying members of the bourgeoisie and one who is fortunately still escaping it, he now, -Vernon that is- is having frequent relapses into his youth. What is worrying his sons however is that Vernon is of late having relapses into other people's youths, like Blackbeard's and Vasco Da Gama's and is actually planning to sail to Brazil because he really loves to samba. When he is not suffering from these delusions he can actually be a pretty nice guy. In his more sane moments, he composes great works of music which he will allow no one to hear and writes little books like this in order to finance his trip to Brazil and to buy another cassette so he won't have to listen to Wayne Newton anymore.

WHAT OTHERS SAY

Will Vernon ever write a book about kite flying?

Elias Vernikos

You mean he didn't drown this summer?

One of his ex-wives

Has anyone suggested that he should take up sky diving, preferably without a parachute? If not, let me do it.

A close associate

I'm sure glad he's getting better at typing but will he ever learn to computer? That surely would be a relief.

Anastasia

Vernon writes them faster than I can read them. I'm still not done with the one he gave me last year.
I only like to read the ''about the author'' section anyway.

Mandy Watkins

What's the matter with Wayne Newton anyway?
I really like him.

His father

OTHER BOOKS BY THE SAME GUY

A FRACTURED LEXICON 1&2
Greek as you've never seen it before.

**A VISITOR'S GUIDE TO MODERN GREEK
BEHAVIOUR AND HABITS**
A must survival guide

**A VISITOR'S GUIDE TO GREEK DRIVING AND
OTHER OXYMORA AND PARADOXA**
Another must guide if you are going to walk around

GREECE WITHOUT TEARS
For the non touristy tourist

GREEK DRAMA
An extremely unorthodox approach

HOW NOT TO SAIL THE GREEK ISLES
For the sailboater and ferryboater alike

DO NOT MISS

SEX

AS A SECOND LANGUAGE

A MODEST ATTEMPT TO
MAKE IT THE FIRST

BY
VERNON AND VERNA ELLIOTT

NOW AVAILABLE